MW01295813

TO CLIMB

THE

HIGHEST MOUNTAIN

by

Greg Woznick

with

A Message of Love

by

Mereece Woznick

To Climb the Highest Mountain

Copyright, 1983
by
Greg Woznick

2013 Edition Produced
by
Bear Woznick
Cover by
Shane Woznick

BEAR'S FORWARD TO THE 2013 EDITION

At the age of 57 my father wrote as he autographed his book to me:

"Strong and Enduring One: Bless you for being a special person and a special son to me. Thank you for your encouragement to write this book, for keeping focused on its vision of "Possibility." You are unique in all the world. Go ahead – Climb the **High**est Mountain – You are extraordinary " – Dad

I found myself at the age of 57, the same age my Dad was when he wrote this book, working hard to meet the publishing deadline for my own first book "**Deep** in the Wave – A Surfing Guide to the Soul." So often I realized how the words in Dad's book and the example of his life challenged me to aim **High** as well as to go **Deep**.

When Dad looks at me incredulously and asks me things like "What were you thinking when you rode your bicycle across the USA, or surfed 24 foot waves, or paddled the treacherous Molokai channel?" I always just say "It's your fault." My problem is that I believed the pages of this book. I could never be satisfied just living inside the box of my comfort zone.

Dad challenges us in this book to live life to the fullest. Dad challenges us to change the trajectory of our lives and to choose our own life script, to seek out our deepest desires and combine them with our gifts and pursue the life purpose that God has called us to.

When you pick up this book you will not put it down until you are done reading it. But you will never be done reading it. You will find yourself returning to it again and again for inspiration.

Bear Woznick

Author of "Deep in the Wave – A Surfing Guide to the Soul"

We expect to add a guest blog from Dad to my website from time to time so you can subscribe at: www.BearsWave.Com

Contact Greg through me at: Bear@BearsWave.Com

Radio: BlogTalkRadio/BearsWave

Twitter: @BearsWave

Facebook: BearsWave.Com

Youtube: BearsWave

"You far seeing, clear sighted Eagle.
You have become a symbol of freedom in your
powerful yet calm soaring flight.

Your overcoming strength drawn from adaptability,
alertness and disciplined resourcefulness.

You, creature of the sky, remind us of our Creator and
our high calling to excellence."

Mereece L. Woznick

It would please me to be YOUR ENCOURAGER.
To point out your potential. . . To encourage you in your dreams and desires. . .To encourage you in your pursuit of excellence. . . To help you *"Climb the Highest Mountain."*

TO CLIMB THE HIGHEST MOUNTAIN

To Mereece

My special bride of sixty-one years I dedicate these few pages which in some small measure represent our life together. For her belief in me, her willingness to "step out", her encouragement for me to follow my dreams. Most of all — for being a loving wife.

CHAPTER 1

"Freddie, what does your daddy do?" asked the third grade teacher.

Freddie sat straight in his chair, squared his shoulders, puffed out his chest and — with a sparkle of pride — answered, "My daddy can do anything. . . He can climb the highest mountain. . . .write the greatest book. . . .fly the fastest plane. . . .catch the biggest fish. . .and ride the meanest horse."

"But, mostly, my daddy just takes out the garbage."

For the past fifteen years my career has been devoted to helping people realize that they can:

> climb the highest mountain
> write the greatest book
> fly the fastest plane
> catch the biggest fish
>   or
> ride the meanest horse;

That they have great potential. And they can do just about anything that they really decide to do.

I am often saddened by and have great compassion for the many wonderful people I meet who are so busy taking out the garbage. Yet, what a great sense of joy and elation I feel when I see how eager and enthusiastic people are to become mountain climbers – to see them break free into a re-birth of purpose. It is thrilling to watch their excitement and confidence as they become aware of who they are, and aware of what they can become.

What holds some back to live a life-time in the squalor of mediocrity while some become free of the restraining shackles to pursue and achieve their dreams and visions?

There are two major limiting factors that keep us shackled from all we can be in life. First, the *perception* I *have of myself*. Second, a *lack of purpose in my life*. Given proper guidance in these two areas, I can:

> become what I want to become
> go where I want to go
> see what I want to see
> do what I want to do

I really can *climb whatever mountain* I *choose to climb.*
There are no limiting factors of age
> or past failure
> or present conditions

Age is not a factor. A man came to me for counsel saying he would really like to return to the University of Minnesota and complete his law degree. My question was if he really wanted to do this – was it personally important to him?

"Yes it really is," he said.

"Why?"

He became very excited and animated, "I've always wanted to be an attorney. It has always been my dream."

"Great! What's the problem, then. Is it money? Can't you get into the program?"

"No. I'm thinking I'm a little old to start over again. My only problem is that I am already thirty years old. I'll be thirty-three when I complete the program."

"How old will you be in three years if you don't go back to school?" I asked.

That was the end of the discussion. Three years later this man returned to his community and successfully launched his life's ambition. He is providing a needed and valuable service to the people in his locality. But most of all, he is living his dream.

Past failures don't count. A few years past, I was hurrying trough the airport in Portland, Oregon. I heard my name being called and turned to see who it was. A well dressed man of fifty was running to catch up with me. He said, "You don't know me, but I was in your audience in San Francisco almost a year ago. I have wanted to thank you for turning my life around."

With this he reached in his shirt pocket and pulled out a dollar bill that had been torn into fragments and scotch-taped back together. Then I remembered that as a closing challenge to that audience, I had held up a dollar bill, and reminded them that their life, like that dollar had real spendable value. "Even so," I had said, "You will decide what it was worth now. And you will decide what its worth would become." It all depended on how they used it.

Then I tore the dollar bill in half because they had already lived out a part of their lives. That part had already been spent. Throwing the one-half dollar on the floor, I challenged them to decide what they were going to do with the part remaining.

They could choose to invest it wisely by using it to become even greater than they were.

To become more loving, more caring, more giving.

To achieve more of the desired things in life.

Or. . . .

They could choose to spend it foolishly, to waste it. No one gets up in the morning with a deliberate intent to fail. Remember, we do not intentionally spend our lives foolishly. . . .or throw away our life's dreams.

No one deliberately spends his life in bitterness, and anger, and frustration.

No one intentionally spends his life's value in loneliness or despair. . . .or hopelessness. Who would willingly spend himself in the self-pity that leads to depression and guilt – and eventually emotional paralysis?

Yet, many become mired in the quicksand of defeat and failure. No, we do not deliberately throw our lives away. Nor do we waste it in large chunks of time. We lose life's value in little time segments of moments – little

4

minutes called procrastination. Procrastination is simply unkept promises to ourselves; Unkept promises to our loved ones; Unkept promises to the other precious people in our lives.

This procrastination is so deviously disguised that it may go on undetected for years. It is as silent as rust. It destroys our life. It eats away at our dreams. But there are some tell-tale signe, that the rust of failure is eroding our lives. Statements that can alert us to its work. Each one tears off a piece of that dollar.

"Someday, I'm really going to get started."

"Someday, I'm really going to get it together."

"Someday, I'm going to be the kind of person you always believed me to be."

"Someday, I'm going to take the time to be a father to my children."

"Someday, I'm even going to church."

"Someday, I'm going to stop drinking."

"Someday, we are going to take that vacation."

"Someday, I'm going to buy you that new refrigerator."

"Someday, I'm going to ask your mother to forgive me."

"Someday, I'm going to buy you that new home."

"Someday, I'm going to climb the highest mountain."

And someday. . . .and someday....and someday....We don't

Know when that will be...

But there will be a day. There will come a final moment when it will be over. We will look back over the fullness – or the debris – of our life and will either say...

"I have no regrets, I have lived a full and richly blessed life. I have loved...and cared...and given...and grown. I have lived my dreams. I wouldn't spend my life any other way."

Or, we will say..."I didn't know it would be over so soon. If only I had it to live over again."

"I would spend it differently."

"I would not have left so many unfulfilled promises t myself or to the people I love."

"I would have stepped out, taken some risks."

"I would have followed my dreams."

"I would have used more of my God-given potential."

Then, blowing the pieces of procrastination into the air and watching them sink to the floor, my closing comment was...

"I B-L-E-W it."

This man went on to say, "When I heard your talk, I was down and out. I had lost my job, my family, and my pride. I was drinking and lonely. I had given up. After everyone had left the auditorium, I snuck back in and down on my knees I gathered u the fragmented and torn pieces of that dollar bill." Standing in that busy airport, crying unashamedly, he confessed, "Each time I picked up a torn piece of that bill from the dirty floor it was like picking up the torn and fragmented pieces from the gutter of my life." Making a fist, he went on, "I clutched them in my hand and cried out to God to help me put the pieces of my life back together."

By now we were both crying. He told me he went home that night to a lonely apartment in Berkely, his self-made prison, and spread out the torn pieces of the dollar on his little kitchen table. As he taped them back together, he mentally began to put the broken pieces of his own life puzzle back into place.

His voice changed to one of sober confidence as he finished his story. "I decided then and there that I would put the pieces of my life back together. That this really was the first day of the rest of my life...That what had happened to me in the past didn't count if I decided to change. That with God's help I *could* decide, for myself what my life was going to be and how I would 'spend' it."

My new friend told me that he has carried that taped up dollar bill in his pocket every day as a reminder to himself that life was a matter of choice – not chance—and that he thanked God for hearing his cry in the auditorium that night. I assured him that Jesus would not extinguish the smallest light of hope and that God was in the prayer answering business.

He said he had never been happier. He had a well paying and responsible position! His family was together in a new and loving relationship. And most of all, now he had re-newed purpose for his life.

Present security is not necessarily ultimate in growth.

Growing up in the small coal mining community of Wilton, North Dakota during the "Great Depression" and living on the out-skirts of town, we raised chickens, pigs, a milking cow and also gardened for much of our food supply. This experience had a way of forging the need for security into a young and developing life concept. Through it all I was blessed with a vivid imagination that spawned many dreams into reality.

Being the youngest of nine children born to immigrant parents in a small restrictive world of hand-me-downs and left-overs did little to enhance my self confidence. I learned, however, that dreams and goals were bigger than security needs and low self-esteem.

For nineteen years I lived and enjoyed my first dream of being a successful coach, teacher and school administrator. My career was rewarding to me and yet it became restricting for me. Financially I had grown weary of saying, "No," to my bride and family when requests were made for even some of the common needs and desires. I became...sick and tired of being...sick and tired. More than that I became frustrated with the empty prose of procrastination...

"Someday honey........"

I left the imprisoned tenured security of my position to set aside the "somedays" and pursued my dreams for growth and a fuller life style. I entered a world that was very strange to me...the world of business. I was fearful. Yet the overpowering magnetism of my dreams provided the drive to overcome the obstacles of fear and uncertainty. *You must give yourself permission to fail in order to give yourself permission to succeed*...all life and venture is risk. Life is mundane.... humdrum.... secure.... and even stale without the willingness to walk on the edge. We must exercise our right to fail *boldly*.

In a few months I developed a successful and profitable distributorship marketing personal and professional development programs for Success Motivation Institute, Inc. Having developed a viable business I set my goal to become a member of the home office staff. That goal was quickly realized and I was invited to become a sales director for that firm. A short while later I became Vice-president of Sales and Marketing. It was here that many dreams were awakened...worked for... and achieved.

And yet... always present in me was the heart of a little boy. A little boy whose dream and yearning to be independent and to enjoy living in a wilderness country... with the freedom of a forest and lake at my door step became very much alive. I set a goal to find wilderness property. Two years later I found it in the Northwoods country of Minnesota in the Chipewa National Forest near the logging community of Longville.

We again left the security of position and status to pursue yet another dream. We moved to this area and opened a retail store. I began a full time career of speaking, consulting and advising individuals and companies on the pursuit of excellence. I was *free* to do what I enjoyed most... helping people to be and become more than they are... to live a life filled with growth... expectation and realization.

GREG WOZNICK

Many of those have asked me to write down these principals for them to keep. A book for reference and encouragement. That writing became a goal – and this book is the result.

Recently a vice-president of a large corporation was sitting on our deck, breathing in the fresh pine scented air... visually drinking in the serenity of the lake and the quiet beauty of the forest. "Greg," he said, "you are one of the very few people I know who has dared to live his dream."

Shortly after we moved to this lovely area, a gentleman called to say how pleased he was to have found that I was living in Northern Minnesota. He had heard my message at the Chanhassen Theatre House just outside the Twin Cities. "In fact", he said "I have heard you twice."

"After I heard you talk on Goal Setting the first time, I became so excited about doing something greater with my life and I knew that my real goal was to start my own business. So I wrote that goal down and put the paper in a desk drawer.

"I looked at my secure position, my good income, my fine marriage. I knew that I was locked into a corporation with no place to grow. But even though I took that written goal out of my desk drawer to read it once in a while, my determination was gone.

Then I heard you were in the community again, and I came to hear you a second time. After the program, I went straight to my office and wrote a letter of resignation. I borrowed $5,000.00 and I started my own business."

Today he operates a multi-million dollar business and is highly respected in his service profession. He owns his own large office complex and other substantial pieces of real estate. Most important of all, he is still growing and setting higher goals.

Anyone who wants to do better
> can do better
> if she/he wants to do better,

regardless of age.... background.... past failures.... or present circumstances. These are the stories of a few of the people who have proven that.

This is a book for every person who really cares about himself – who desires a brighter and more rewarding future. Any person who is willing to take the first step to make that future happen.

This book will help you to see what a wonderful person you are right now, and how much more wonderful you can become. It will re-kindle a peaceful and joyful desire for life and inspirational discontent with things as they are. You will find purpose and meaning in living. And you will become confident and assured that the direction you choose for your life will be the right one.

I offer no panaceas... no magic formulas... no "latest in the world of trends and instant solutions".

These principles, concepts and ideas are simple

> proven
> workable
> effective
> and get results.

So let's get on with it.
Let's talk about you.

Let us make man
in our own image.
*   -- God*

CHAPTER 2

What is your personal net-worth? No, I am not referring to your financial statement. I am referring to something far, far more valuable and of much greater importance than the most impressive financial net worth.

I am referring to *you* – personally. What do you think you are worth? Not what others think you're worth, but what you think you're worth. We spend so much of our time trying to... be perfect... hurry up... try hard and please others, trying to be the sort of person we think they want us to be. We forget to please ourselves and appreciate our own greatness.

If you spend your time trying to be OK and to please others, you will not have the time left over to please yourself. You are important! In this whole world you are the only one other than God who will never leave you; you are the only one you can really count on.

So what are you worth? The answer is simple. You are worth whatever you decide you are worth... whatever value you place on yourself. This perception of yourself determines how much you will give to life,

how much happiness you will enjoy and

how much you will really achieve.

This perception of yourself is called *self-worth*. What your life will be one year, five years, or ten years from now totally depends on what you think you are now – and what you think you can become. The difference between those two points, the way you see yourself now and what you think you can become is called *growth potential*. We'll discuss *growth potential* later; first how do you evaluate your own self-worth?

Let's take a moment and assess your personal net worth as you perceive it right now.

On a scale from 1 to 10, how do you feel about yourself? A 1 means that you don't like yourself. Perhaps you feel you are emotionally, spiritually or financially bankrupt and don't like who you are, or what you are becoming. You may even feel a bit plastic or phony – as if to say, "Well, I know I'm not all that good, but I have other people fooled. They really think I'm better than I actually am."

The me I think I am.
The me I think other
People see me as.

Or, do you feel like a 10? Do you like who you are and what you are becoming? You might say, "I have a couple of character deficiencies that need correcting." Or, "I have a relationship problem at home or on the job, but, by golly, I'm working on them ... I do feel like a ten."

Go ahead, give yourself a number. It's a beginning.

During the first morning of a Management Training Seminar outside Seattle, I asked a group of regional vice-presidents to rate themselves on this same scale of 1-10. I had suggested that they could keep their answers personal, but the *espirit de corps* was such that they began to shout out their answers.

"I'm a seven!"

"I'm a six!"

"I'm an eight!"

So it went back and forth across the conference table.

No tens.

No tens!

As we continued in the program, I noticed that one man was lost in thought and not paying attention. I wondered how to tactfully get him back into the discussion without embarrassing him. A few minutes later Sam looked up at me and I could see that his mind was refocusing on the present discussion.

He politely raised his hand to ask if he could interrupt. I quickly said, "of course." I was glad to have his attention back with us. Sam looked straight into my eyes.

"I have been thinking about your question of how we felt about ourselves on a scale from 1-10." There was a long breathless pause. The total attention of that executive group was fixed on Sam. I broke through the growing anxiety of silence. "Sam, I'm glad you took that question seriously. Do you want to share the number you think you are? Remember, you are not expected to tell us."

Sam's face turned a shade pink as he shuffled his anxiety into a more comfortable position, stammering, "No, I don't mind." I felt uncomfortable for Sam and reminded him, "You really aren't expected to share your number with us, Sam."

With this Sam's face turned beet red. The hair on the back of his neck began to bristle. He held his breath for a moment, then blurted out, "I think I'm a *nine!*"

I remember the shocked look on the faces of his friends. His peers. Do you think they said, "That's great Sam, we believe in you, you bet you're a nine! Keep growing Sam, be a ten!"?

Or, do you think they said, "Come on, Sam, be realistic. You're not a nine, you're a seven – or even a six, at the most, you're an eight! Get down here with the rest of us."?

Well from your own experience, you probably guessed correctly. They laughed a "good-natured" laugh. But that laugh was cutting and painful. It was ridicule. And they did what some people did to you when you were in school – or perhaps even yesterday.

They laughed at him.

They put him down.

They tore huge chunks out of his personal net worth. The real tragedy of this story, however, is that the group was absolutely correct.

Sam was not a nine.

Sam was a ten!

And you are a ten...

Because God made you... and He doesn't make junk.

He never has, and He never will. He said that He created you in His image and in His likeness. That you were to have dominion over the birds of the air, and the animals of the earth, and the fish of the sea. He said that you were His child and, since He is a King, you are a King's Kid.

God is not in the business of making counterfeits or imitations. He deals only in unique and beautiful originals. There is no other person like YOU. You are great! You are special! You are precious! You are very *worthwhile.*

"If what you say is true," you ask "then why do I feel like a five, or a six, or a seven or an eight? Why don't I feel like a ten?" Psychology has a term that explains that feeling. It's called "objective reality."

"Objective reality" means that if you are told something often enough you will accept it as the truth even though it is not true. Or, as another example, it is not uncommon for two people to witness a car accident and then report two different sets of circumstances leading up to the impact. We know that there is only one factual way this accident occurred. And that may even be different than what either of the two witnesses say. The witness' viewpoint in this is called *objective reality*. The factual events of the accident make up the Reality. Your objective reality may say you are a six, but the REALITY AND THE TRUTH ABOUT YOU IS THAT YOU ARE A TEN.

At birth you receive an inheritance for greatness. This greatness, though freely given, must be accepted and then developed and exercised. You have tremendous God-given talent and potential within yourself ready and available for use. You must be the one to decide its use and value.

Consider the magnificence of your mind — a three pound mass of cells.

- Your mind is comprised of ten billion-billion working parts.
- You speak the equivalent of one full novel each day.
- It has been estimated that if it were possible to duplicate the "known" functions of the brain into computer systems, it would take a building the size of the Empire State Building to house it. All the water coming over Niagara Falls would be needed to power it and cool it. And yet this imitation would not be able to cry ... or laugh ... or love ... or care ... or give ... or grow.

In the Sequoia National Park stands a giant redwood tree called the General Sherman tree. It is a gigantic tree, alive and flourishing — still growing to reach its full potential. Still striving to become all the God has intended it to be.

> That tree stands 278 feet tall with a diameter of 107 feet. It would take seventeen men to reach around it finger-tip to finger-tip. One hundred and thirty feet above the ground is a branch that is seven feet in diameter, stretching out 235 feet into space. There is enough lumber in that tree to build 500 three-bedroom bungalows, and would require 330 railroad flatcars to carry it away.

You cannot look up into that tree without realizing that if God put so much potential for growth and giving into a tree, how much more must he have given to you, and to me.

Your potential is limitless. You can be what you want to be.

Become what you want to become.

See what you want to see.

Have what you want to have.

Go where you want to go.

YES YOU CAN!

Check it out:

- Can you climb the highest mountain? ... Could you if you wanted to?

- Can you write a book? ... Could you if you wanted to?

- Can you fly a plane? ... Could you if you wanted to?
- Can you catch fish? ... Could you if you wanted to?
- Can you speak Spanish, Ukrainian, German? ... Could you if you wanted to?
- Can you ski? ... Could you if you wanted to?
- Can you bake a delicious pie? ... Could you if you wanted to?
- Can you travel around the world? ... Could you if you wanted to?
- Can you move your family into that new home? ... Could you if you wanted to?
- Can you take that dream vacation? ... Could you if you wanted to?
- Can you be a better husband – wife – father – mother? ... Could you if you wanted to?

Or, are you like Freddie's father?

Do you mostly just take out the garbage.

You could make an endless list of things to see ... to do ... to have... to become. And you could write a YES behind almost every one of them...

IF YOU WANTED TO.

"But," you say, "*I've always wanted to.* What is stopping me?"

There are two major hindrances
Emotional Blocks
Inability to see our
own potential.

I'm glad we have emotions. I'm glad we have feelings.
It's good that we can laugh
and sing
and love
and care
and yes it's even good that we can hurt
and have compassion.

"Well," you say, "if emotions are so good and we should be glad to have them, why are they often an obstacle to my doing what I want to do?"

The answer is as simple as it is important. Our emotions often interfere with our intellect in making decisions. Our emotions frequently control our behavior even when we prefer that they didn't. Frequently we find our emotions pulling us in the direction opposite of our logic or good common sense.

LOGIC ← DECISIONS → EMOTIONS

This situation results in damaging our self-worth, because we often do the inappropriate thing and then "condemn ourselves" or "feel guilty" for doing it. Too often, we know what we should do – but emotionally we cannot release ourselves to do it.

There are emotional blocks that limit our actions.

Reluctance:

A sales person knows that she must make a certain number of phone calls every day in order to make enough appointments. Logically she knows this is true. She knows that this is imperative in order to maintain her income level.

Yet, emotionally she may not be able to make the calls because of an emotional block called *reluctance*.

Managers admit to me that one of their most difficult responsibilities is dealing with problem employees. They know intellectually how important it is for them to correct a behavior or attitude pattern in an employee. But, even knowing the seriousness of the situation, that manager procrastinates to avoid an "uncomfortable" situation. On the way home from work, he may make up all sorts of speeches to a rebellious employee. And at that time, will have the complete determination to follow through. But he is usually quick to admit that on the way to work in the morning, the old emotions set in that cause him to again shrink from his acknowledge responsibility. So day after day, the manager feels less and less competent. *His* self-worth diminishes, as he grows increasingly unable to accept his responsibility and becomes increasingly ineffectual.

Pride:

A husband may be rude or angry or ungrateful toward his wife and leave her feeling hurt as he goes to work. He knows logically that he needs to ask her for forgiveness. But emotionally, his pride keeps him from doing the appropriate thing to restore his most valued relationship.

We can list example after example of the problems this condition creates for us. We feel:

anger
  self-pity
    blameful
      blameless

righteous

withdrawn

It is a self-defeating and demoralizing condition. It draws away our energy. It causes us to vacillate in the decisions of our lives. It can cause depression. It frustrates our dreams. It keeps us forever on an emotional teeter-totter. We feel as though we are being "ripped apart".

The symptoms are not always obvious. They sometimes disguise themselves in expressions like:

"Well, that's life."

"I guess I'm doing okay, everybody's got problems these days."

"I have a pretty good job ... got security and a paid vacation. I guess I can live though it."

"You gotta take the good with the bad."

"Life is no bowl of cherries."

"Boy, with my dumb luck."

"Someday honey, I'm really gonna get started."

"I guess things are okay the way they are. We don't need much."

Listen to yourself. Are you making these or similar statements? *Please* protect your net worth. Each time you yield to this sort of thinking, you tear out a chunk of your self.

It is obvious that emotions either control us, or we control our emotions. Emotions are neither automatic nor uncontrollable... emotions are feelings we *allow* ourselves to have. We *can* control our emotions, our attitudes in any given circumstance or condition...

if we choose to.

Emotions, properly directed are constructive qualities of the personality, provided they compliment and harmonize with the intellect, to help you give life what YOU WANT. Emotions are constructive when there is unity of purpose and commitment in your life.

In other words, we need to get our logic and emotions traveling in the same direction.

LOGIC →

EMOTION →

As we do this we find that "who I am as a person" and "what I do," are compatible. This relationship between logic and emotion will not happen by accident. You must have purpose and goals for your life that will bring your logic, emotions and spirit into harmony.

LOGIC →

DESIRE → GOALS

EMOTION →

You now have a simplified illustration of a "mountain climbing" self-motivated person. A person whose life and emotions are reinforcing to each other. This is a person who has purpose and goals for his life. This is an individual who recognizes that desire is a healthy, productive, emotional appetite essential for the attainment of dreams and goals.

We are looking at a person who recognizes that life is a matter of choice not chance. We are looking at you ... the way you are now ... and , the way you are going to be.

Seeing and Believing our Own Potential:

Sometimes we can't really see our own potential. Even though we know the facts about what God has done in nature or in someone else, we can't apply it to our lives and break it down so we can grow from it. We often need an outside source to do this. I hope this book will be one of the sources, but the most valuable source is someone who believes in us and can show us how to believe in ourselves. We need an encourager.

The development of your own identity must be encouraged. It takes someone who can objectively see our lives in the positive and can then *tell* us what they see in us. That takes a strong – caring person. Someone who is not threatened by another's achievements. Someone able to look through his own filters of past and present to see the possibilities in us. Such a perception is rare, and such a friend is a real gift.

I am continually amazed when I ask an audience, "How many people in your entire life have ever expressed a deep belief in you and your ability? Consider all the people you know – parents, brothers, sisters, teachers, ministers, neighbors, friends. How many of them ever spoke to a special part of you and said something like ...

Cindy, I think you are one of the loveliest and greatest persons I have ever known. I see in you such a capacity for greatness. I see in you such ability and potential ... I see a giant in you – waiting to stretch out and get moving... If you could see yourself right now as I see you, you'd be fantastic." They might have used different words, but that's the message.

How many people ever said something like this and gave you hope and confidence, and a new belief in yourself? Encouragement that caused you to stand tall and make a decision

> to be
>
> to become
>
> to grow
>
> to see
>
> to do.

How many? Would you need all the fingers on both hands to count them?

It is a sad commentary that, with few exceptions, most of the audience members can come up with no more than three. Many who have said five or more, when asked to specifically name them, suddenly realize how few people have encouraged them to become all they really could be.

During a convention of School Administrators in Bismarck, North Dakota, I asked the audience of over three hundred professionals the same question.

They gave the expected responses of "three" and occasional "four". I told them that in my entire life, only four people had ever reached inside me to help me believe in myself.

Looking past the glaring stage lights as I said this, I spotted someone. Someone very special. Jack Moreland.

The lump in my throat grew as I said to that audience, "One of my four fingers is sitting here in the auditorium today. Would it be okay if I asked him to stand?"

"Yes!" with a huge applause.

"In that case, Jack Moreland, would you please stand up so I can publically thank and bless you for what you meant to a poor, Ukrainian coal miner's kid?"
Jack stood up humbly and slowly. And, as the whole audience rose to give him a standing ovation, Jack began to sob, tears running – un-wiped – down his cheeks and onto his suit.

During lunch with Jack and his wife that day, I asked, "Jack didn't you know how you influenced my life? Didn't you know that you helped me to see that it was not necessary to spend my life in the symbolic darkness of a soggy coal mine?"

"No." he answered, "I didn't know. I only knew that I saw in you someone who – given a chance – could do something special with his life."

A few weeks later I received a phone call, Jack had died during a hunting trip. I thought, "What if I hadn't thanked Jack before he passed away?" I sat down at the next possible moment and began writing notes of appreciation to the many others who had helped me in some way to believe in myself.

Just like Jack, you can put your own fingerprint of being on the souls of those you touch. It is more blessed to give than to receive.

An encourager is important to help you see your potential. God also wants to be our encourager. It is in His very nature. When there is no one else around to encourage you, read the love letter he left you; the Bible. But there is something even more important than the amount of encouragement you have had. It is important to determine who you are – to define

the inner desires of your heart

the attitudes of your life value system and outlook

the potential of growth in all areas of your life.

There are ways to do it.

Seek and you shall find.

CHAPTER 3

The compass really has 5 points. North, South, East, West – and where you are standing. You can only know where you are going, and how you will get there, if you know where you are standing right now.

Suppose you drove to Northern Minnesota and called my home saying, "Greg, I'm in your area and would like to come by to see you. How do I get there?"

I would ask, "Where are you now?" We call that answer a *realistic appraisal.*

WHERE ARE YOU STANDING NOW in our scale of 1-10? What you thought of yourself – your own evaluation – is called your self-worth. Often our answer is contaminated because we confuse who we are with what we do. Let's get rid of the muddle so we can deal with each concept separately.

Who you are as a person, the real honest to goodness you on the inside where you live, we call your *self-image identity.* These are the characteristics that make up *you.* What you do in life, the actions and responsibilities you perform we will call *Roles*.

We play dozens and dozens of roles every day. You are perhaps a husband, wife, father, mother, son, daughter, car driver, golfer, swimmer, student, manager, salesperson, and on, and on.

Mostly we are judged by our roles. Society pays far more attention and gives greater recognition to what we do than to what we are... Do you believe it? Test it... We can observe this in the introduction of people. We say ...

"I would like to have you meet Mary Brown, Mary is a third grade teacher at the local school."

"This is Dick Tater. Dick is the foreman out at the plant."

"Or, as we introduce ourselves we might say, "Hi, my name is Jim Nasium, I'm the basketball coach. What is your name, and what do you do?" These are examples of *Role Introductions*.

How often, if ever have you heard an introduction in which someone might say, "I would like you to meet a great gal, Dawn. She is one of the most generous, giving, and caring persons I have ever known." This is an *Identity Introduction*.

We can now understand the difference between Identity and Roles, and we have already given ourselves a rating in our identity. There is also a way to make a realistic appraisal of where we now stand in the roles we play.

As we do this, keep in mind that the kind of person you perceive yourself to be – your self-image identity – will greatly determine how well you play out the roles in your life. Your self-image limits or releases your expectations of yourself and your future achievements.

We are saying, then, that in the center of your life is *you*. Your *identity evaluation* forms the hub of your life, with the roles going out from this core as the spokes on a wheel of life.

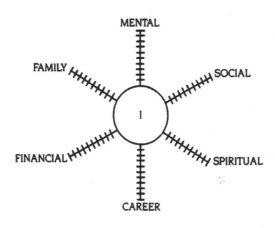

As we consider the major roles we play in life, how will you rate yourself on a scale form 1-10? At first this may be difficult – but it will really be worth the effort.

HOW ARE YOU DOING IN YOUR:

Family Life

Is your family important to you?

Do they know it?

How does your family feel when *you* come home at night?

How does your family feel when *they* come home at night?

Do you see your family as a nuisance?

Are you anxious to have the children grown up and gone?

When did you last tell "each" one of them that you loved them?

Do you talk to them in "life-giving" constructive words and tones or death-giving words?

Do you see their events and concerns as important?

Do your *actions* show your love for them?

Social Life

Do you have at least two or three friends close enough to share your special concerns?

Are you considered polite and mannerly?

Are you a good neighbor ... respectful, helpful?

Do you see personal correspondence as important?

Financial Life

Are you a good steward with your money and possessions?

Do you keep things in good repair?

Do you meet your obligations on time?

Are you careful not to go into debt for items that depreciate such as autos and appliances?

Are you saving a part of what you earn on a consistent basis?

Have you taken ample steps to provide for your family should you die?

Do you keep a spending budget? Do you use it to control unnecessary spending?

Spiritual Life

Is this important to you?

Are you leaving this aspect to a more convenient time?

Are you attending a church or synagogue regularly?

Do you believe Jesus Christ died for your sins?

Do you believe it is important to commit your life to the lordship of Jesus Christ?

Do you believe in a life-here-after?

If you died today, are you certain you would go to heaven? If not, will you seek answers to this question?

Are you afraid to die?

Physical Life

Is good physical health important to you?

Is good health important to the members of your family?

Would you enjoy each other more if you were healthy and energetic?

Do you come home to "too pooped to play"?

If physical health is important to you, when was your last physical checkup ... your last dental checkup?

When did you last get five good night's sleep in a row?

Are you eating a well-balanced diet?

Are you avoiding too much salt in your food?

Do you smoke?

Are you taking drugs other than prescription drugs?

Do you drink to feel right or good?

Mental Life

Are you reading constructive magazines?

Do you listen to the News?

Are you inquisitive?

Are you interested in any special area – history, archeology, science, business, computers, art?

Are you a good listener?

What books have you read this year?

Do you cultivate interesting friends?

Positive friends?

Are you aware of your psychological needs?

Career Life

Are you enthused about your work?

Do you try to be?

Do you feel negative or positive about going to work?

Do you believe you are giving your employer a full day's work for a full day's pay?

Are you loyal and submissive to your superiors?

Do you murmur and complain to other employees at breaks or in the parking lot?

Do you see your role as helping your boss, and your company, succeed?

What have you done in the last three months to improve yourself in your job?

What are your improvement goals for the next year?

Certainly we could ask many, many more questions in each area; these are just 'prompters'. Go ahead and add to the list of questions. But for right now, rate yourself in each category... Do it now, before you go on.

Finished?...... Fine... now go back to the Identity-Role illustration and mark on the spoke of each role to indicate the score you gave yourself.

That's great, thank you... Now... Please connect the dots. Did you make a perfect circle? Did you make a large or small circle? Did it form a well-rounded wheel of life, or did it look something like this?

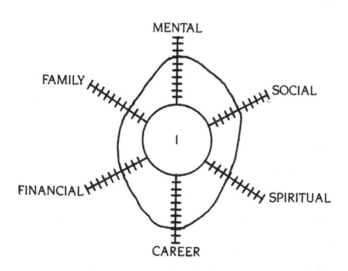

However it looks... it's okay! What we *have done* with our lives is not as important as what we *will do* with our lives from this day forward. Today IS a new day. Today IS the first day of the rest of your life. HAPPY BIRTHDAY!

You have established the fifth point in your life's compass. You have taken a *realistic appraisal*. Now you know where you stand. In the next chapters you will learn how to make "all things new". How to set exciting... rewarding... reachable goals in each of those areas. You will develop a profile of an even more successful and goal directed... self-motivated *you.*

Before we leave this illustration, ask yourself this question. How much of my time has been spent learning to become a better "role player" compared to the time I have spent becoming a better person? My research indicates that most people spend about ninety-five percent of their time learning more about roles. That leaves only 5% of their time to devote to becoming a better person – the characteristics that make up their real identity. Since what you are as a person determines how well you perform the roles in your life, then perhaps these percentages need to be reversed!

Now that we have an understanding of what is meant by self-image identity and what is meant by roles, it is important that we view them in their proper relationship. We need to be able to identify their effect on our actions and decision making process. In your experience as a supervisor or a committee coordinator, or even in your job, you know how very difficult it is to correct another person's behavior. You want to be "constructive". Yet you are concerned that the person may take it in the "wrong way". So rather than risk being misunderstood, or possible causing hurt, you avoid taking the responsibility to confront that individual. Or, perhaps you say something like, "Listen John, I have been meaning to talk to you about something and... ah... listen, how is your wife... how are the kids?" etc... etc...

If you do get around to having that talk with John you will probably say, "John, I want you to know that I appreciate you and your sense of humor, and I value you as a friend. Now, don't take this personally..." and then we add a destructive three letter word... "BUT...."

Invariable, where will John take it? Although your intention was to speak to him in his *Role*, he will respond to you in his *Identity*. He takes it personally. He leaves feeling hurt. And you are left feeling uncomfortable. The situation may be in a less productive position now than it was before the conversation.

Someone may criticize our work, our cooking, our driving, or any other role we are playing. When that happens... like John, we tend to take it personally. We mentally refer to the comment as a question of our self-worth – our identity – instead of simply a statement or suggestion of improvement in a role we perform. Then our reaction tends to contaminate everything else we do. A husband takes an argument that he had with his wife to work with him... A salesman has difficulty making the next call because of a customer complaint... an accountant begins making errors because he was admonished. A teacher is less effective because of an abusive parent.

Separate your I's from your R's. Look at the comment for what it is. Ask yourself, "Was he justified in making that remark? Is there something I'm doing that I should change? How can that comment make me more productive – more efficient?"

When I can really see a statement about my performance in a role as simply an opportunity to perform that role better – not as an attack against who I am inside – then I *can respond in truth* in a situation. But the key to my response lies in my ability emotionally and mentally to separate my role from my identity. We must separate our identity from our roles in our job, our marriage, and our view of life itself.

There is another way that the ability to separate identity from roles will prevent a lot of self-destruction.

With the rapid increase in job change and job demand, it is increasingly important for us to develop our identity. If we fail to do so, we get the notion that the job is getting "too big for me".

Perhaps when you first started the job you have now, you were a little anxious about it, but you were really excited. Perhaps it was what you really wanted to do. It was exciting because who you were was compatible and congruent with what you were going to do... Your picture looked   like   this

→ → → Identity

→ → → Job-Role

Your I – R Profile was positive and pointed in the same direction, pulling together to give you life and job satisfaction. However, as the demands on your job began to grow, or change, and you failed to keep up with the change in your identity... the "who you are" and the "what you do" began to separate. Your profile may look like this:

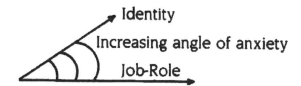

The longer you continue to work at a job that you believe is "bigger" than you – day after day... week after week... month after month, while doing nothing to correct it – you develop what we call an increasing angle of anxiety and frustration. You find yourself re-acting to your work circumstances rather than acting.

An even more devastating and destructive identity and role separation problem occurs when we fail to be enthused about our work, however menial it might be. This creates the opposite effect which is one of an increasing angle of boredom.

Unfortunately, we find both of these examples multiplied in marriages and in all of life itself because we fail to grow. The increasing angle of anxiety and the increasing angle of boredom become self-imposed limitation to our lives, filling our lives with tragedy and despair.

CHAPTER 4

In Physics we learn that the rate of a falling body is sixteen feet per second squared until it reaches maximum velocity. This is called the "law" or the 'principle' of gravity. We accept this as the truth, we believe it and apply it and it works the same way – every time.

Suppose, however. That you were teaching a class this principle of gravity. As you were about to drop a book to demonstrate your point, a creature from outer space appeared and said, "That's nonsense, if you drop that book, it's not going to fall down, it will fall up." Whether this creature believed it or not, which way would the book fall? Of course... it would fall down.

So it is with all the principles of life. Whether you believe them or not, if you apply them, they work for you. Go ahead... drop your book.

And so it is with this next principle. It is more than a principle, it is an absolute − it is a basic truth, a basic building block to all others. As you accept it you will find greater freedom, peace, joy, security and hope than ever before. If you say no, the rest of the book is still valid and important to you... the other principles will still work. But, if you say yes... you will be richer than you ever thought possible.

Looking back at chapter three, we discussed Identity and Role relationships. Remember that our identity is the hub of the wheel... the hub of life, with spokes leading out to the roles we perform. Let's illustrate that picture again.

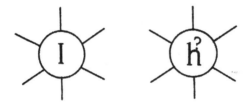

But this illustration is incomplete. If I leave the illustration as it is, then I have said that YOU and only YOU are the center of your life. That you can do it "My Way", as the song goes... that you do not need help... guidance... or anyone to "light" your way. It becomes a picture of the philosophy of *humanism* that would say, "I'm great because I made myself great. I can seek and become perfect on my own".

Something is missing in that illustration... Something that most of us miss until it is pointed out to us. Here is the correction. This will make the illustration complete.

First, let's take the "I" out of the center and replace it with a throne. As you look at that throne, who or what is sitting on the chair in the center of the throne room?... The center of your life... your identity?

Is it low self-image?

Is it debt, a financial problem?

Is a broken relationship sitting there?

Or perhaps self-pity, or depression, or anger, or bitterness?

Or perhaps, it's money or your job.

Or your new car, boat, or the home you're building.

Maybe even one of your children.

Or, are *you* sitting on that throne?

What or who is taking the space at the center of your life; what takes your time, your energy – what holds your thoughts and your life "captive"?

Suppose we put someone else on the throne of our life. Someone so special and so full of love for us that no sacrifice would be too great for him. Someone who said, "I came that you might have life and have it abundantly. I am the truth, and the light, and the way. Anyone who believes in me shall have eternal life." A person who never pushed or argued or insisted that you do it "His way" but simply said, "Follow me".

That invitation is being offered to you today and everyday. Would you turn down an invitation from the governor or the President of the United States to join him for dinner? Of course you wouldn't, you would be excited, thrilled and maybe even a little nervous to accept the invitation.

If we would be so excited over an invitation like that – and be so honored and quick to accept – why wouldn't we feel the same way about accepting an invitation from the King of Kings, the Lord of Lords? How will your RSVP read:

> "Sorry, I have to sell my fatted cow."
>
> "I really don't have much time to think about it right now... I'm pretty well for me right now I'm even building bigger granaries and barns... wouldn't care to get involve right now."
>
> "Look, I lead a good life. I help my neighbor, and work at the church, and pay my dues. Isn't that enough?"
>
> "It would be inconvenient right now... I wouldn't want to change my life style."

Did you hear someone say, "Here I stand knocking at your door. If anyone hears and opens the door, I will come in sand sup with him"? He would never batter your door down... never... He just knocks, gently. He will never insist that you accept the invitation to dine with him. You have a free will to choose whatever way you like. How will your RSVP read?

The question remains, do you want a YOU centered life or a GOD centered life. If you could choose who would make the decisions in your life – you or God –

which would you choose? Which of you has the greatest wisdom?

I asked this question of a group of teenagers recently. Very few wanted to leave their decisions to God. When I asked why... a very honest young man volunteered, "Because, I don't know God well enough to trust him with my life." Sad, but true.

When Jesus said, "Follow me." He was inviting us to be a "follower". To be a follower, I must commit to his leadership. I must commit to his LORDSHIP. Giving up my rights, my property, my family, and yes... even my *problems*. He will take them all. What is His, He watches over and blesses.

How do I do this? How do I develop a God-centered life? Simple. Ask Him. Ask Him to sit on the throne. To take the center stage. Tell Him you want to know Him personally. Go ahead, you can talk to Him. When He is in your life... you *will* know Him personally.

So, go back and place a cross through the I in the illustration. You are on your way to a more beautiful life than you have ever imagined possible.

If anyone is in Christ he is a new creation... that's you... a new creation. He will make all things new. You will be slowly transformed into the image and likeness of Christ himself. With His characteristics of strength, courage, peace, joy, kindness, optimism.

In Him you will become a magnificent *ten* in every way.

CHAPTER 5

As you approach the gate leading to "Eagle's Rest", our lake retreat, you will see a tree that tells a magnificent story of growth and determination. Each time I drive guests to our home, I delight in stopping on the tree lined forest road and pointing that tree out as an example of the strength and innate desire for growth in all living things.

The trunk is seven feet in circumference, and it tops out at about fifty feet with a majestic crown of healthy living branches and leaves. But, at about twenty feet from the ground, the trunk bends completely over and down and runs horizontally for six feet before it juts sunward again.

We can tell that when the oak tree was some seven or eight years old, a rotten tree had fallen across it, placing its total weight on the life of the good tree. The oak bent over and continued to grow, but it was crippled. Yet, when the burden fell away – or when the tree had "outgrown" the problem – it righted itself to become all that God had intended it to be.

There are many lessons in that tree, for we too have the innate desire to grow. Like that tree we are always growing. But the questions is, how are we growing? Are we growing in a crippling and negative fashion? Or, are we growing to become all that we can be? Straight and tall and stately – with a crown of nobility. Like the tree, each of us possesses the inherent ability to right ourselves in any given situation. We can *choose* to allow failure... or guilt... or indecision... to burden us. Just as the rotted tree burdened the live oak. Or like the tree, we can overcome the problem and 'right' ourselves. That choice is always ours.

Many years ago on a driving trip across Montana, I was astounded to see scrub oak growing out of cracks in huge boulders. I was so intrigued that I stopped along the road and climbed up the side of a mountain to examine this impossibility. Looking into the cleft of the boulder I could see part of a bare root system, absorbing what little food and water that became available. Those scrub oak have such a determination to grow that they exert tremendous pressure against the boulder, splitting the huge rocks that confined their growing room.

The natural and powerful growth force in our own lives must be examined through something called the "self". There are two major influences on the development of our "self" – *what is said to us* and *what we say to ourselves*. This "self" is a divine potency that has been built since life began in the womb of your mother. You have been shaped by experience unique to you on a biological structure that is uniquely yours. Although "self" is not the appearance of physical features – like blond hair or blue eyes – our concept of self will affect our response to those features of the world around us.

We certainly recognize the significant influences of environment, church, school, inherited qualities and many other forces in the shaping of our lives and personalities. Although each of these factors contributes to – or detracts from – my growth, the most important impact on life development comes from my relationship with others around me.

As a newborn we were equipped for growth, but could not develop in the absence of others. What others said to us, and how it was said, formed us in those earliest years. We create – or destroy – with our very words. Matthew 12:6 "Every idle word that men shall speak, they shall give an accounting of in the day of judgment."

I *Thessalonians* 5:11, "So give encouragement to each other, and keep strengthening one another, as you do already."

Begin to apply this truth to your life and to the lives of those around you. How many divorces... broken relationships... business failures have resulted from the use of death giving words? How much sorrow... and hurt... and agony has been inflicted by critical, belittling... condemning words?

You will experience a dramatic positive change in your life and the lives of those around you when you practice this principle. Learn to use words like:

"You're wonderful."

"You're great."

"I really appreciate who you are."

"I think you are so wonderfully unusual."

"I believe in you."

"You're special."

"You're important to me."

"I thank God for you."

Train your children in this positive direction. Ask them, "What are the two greatest most wonderful things that happened to you today?" Get them to focus on, and look for, the good around them. Help them to realize that *life will become what they see it to be.* Build them with life-giving words.

We know the story of the man who drove into a rural community to see if he wanted to move his family there. He stopped by a park bench where two old-timers were sitting and questioned, "What sort of people are living in this community? I'm thinking of moving here."

One of the gentlemen asked, "What kind of people live in the town you are in now?"

The man replied, "The people in my town are selfish and stubborn and mean. That's why I want to move."

"Well," said the old-timer, "That's the same kind of people we have living here, too."

A few minutes later, a second car drove up and another man asked the same question.

"What sort of folks live in the town you're in now?"

"Well, in my town we have great people – friendly, giving, caring folks."

"That's that same kind of people we have living in this village," said the old-timer.

As the man drove away, his friend asked, "Why did you give both of them the same answer?"

With the wisdom of age he answered, "Each man will get out of this town whatever he comes looking for." Look for the best... and you will find the best, right where you are.

Be careful what you say, especially to your children. What you say to them now is what they will be saying to themselves and believing about themselves later on. It happened to you; it will happen to them. Build up their personal net-worth. Help them to become exceedingly rich in themselves.

Let me ask you an important question... When you are alone, are you the kind of company you would like to keep? What sort of conversation are you having with yourself? Are your thoughts critical... full of doubt... worry... anger... Are you feeling self-pity? Or, are you happy and positive with thoughts of joy and peach and gratefulness?

Once I was asked, on short notice, to drive to San Antonio to help a business friend. It was early in the evening and I explained to my family that I would need to drive there and back that night.

My teenaged daughter Tammy said, "Gee Dad, I'm sorry you have to take this trip alone, if it weren't for cheerleading practice I would go with you."

She blessed me with her thoughtfulness, but I answered, "Thank you for caring, Tammy, but I won't be driving alone. I will be in great company."

She said, "Oh, who is going with you?"

I replied, "No one, I am going alone, but I promise that I will think great and wonderful thoughts as I am driving."

When we learn to take responsibility for our own lives, it is no longer as important what others say to us as what we say to ourselves. This is a major principle for increasing our net-worth. Proverbs says, "As a man thinketh in his heart, so is he... And as you sow, so shall you reap."

We understand that the conscious mind comprises about one-tenth of the brain capacity; nine-tenths is considered subconscious. The subconscious is the "Heart" into which we sow. Unlike the conscious mind that distinguishes right from wrong – truth from untruth – the subconscious mind receives all messages as *true*. You may say to a little child, "You little dummy," or worse. You may say it in jest. But the subconscious does not receive it as jest. It accepts it as fact, and simply records it as *truth*. What awesome power in our words.

As we sow into the subconscious, it gives back to life whatever the fruit of the seeds that are planted. And it gives it back in multiples, so we have a self-determined harvest of good or bad. If you sow love, you get love back... if you sow hatred, you get hatred back... if you sow despair, you get despair back... if you sow belief, you get belief back.

Proverbs 4:20, "Watch over your heart, for out of it comes all the sources of life."

Block out the negative seed of thought that others might plant. Receive only the good words. PLEASE *plant* only the good. Words of love, caring and belief, and faith in your own heart. **If you love yourself... treat yourself with respect and dignity.**

CHAPTER 6

We imagine that thought can be kept secret, but it cannot. Thought rapidly crystallizes into habit. And habit solidifies into circumstance.

How very powerful is that statement of fact. We are frequently careless with our self-talk. We view it as common... ordinary... unimportant. We fail to recognize the impact that it has on our lives. As the plant springs from the seed and could not be without it, so every act of a person springs from the hidden seed of thought.

The term used for this "self-talk" is called *affirmations*. It is estimated that we spend approximately seventy percent of our time talking to ourselves. Even as you are reading this you are perhaps talking to yourself. You may be agreeing. You may be relating this information to some practical form.

Because of its simplicity we tend to discount its tremendous importance to us. We might hear ourselves saying, "This is too good to be true. Anything that can do that much for me would have to be difficult."

Affirmations are controlled, directed conversations with ourselves. An Affirmation is a statement we make that is presently true about ourselves and we want to continue this truth. Or, it is a statement we make about ourselves that may not be true at the present time but will be true about ourselves if we continue to repeat it.

When I left education and went into business, it was imperative that I personally do a great deal of the selling to get the company going. My personal feelings about being a salesman were very negative. Affirmations like....

"Never trust a salesman."

"Watch out for 'blue suede' salesmen"

"I'm in selling until a 'legitimate job' comes along."

.... were a very "fixed" way of thinking and feeling about selling as a profession. I had a great handicap of thought. It was necessary for me to sell in order to earn a living and yet "everything in me" revolted at this necessity. I was being controlled by previous faulty thinking and conditioning.

My situation was desperate. I had given up a fixed salary, I would receive no income unless I *sold* something. This was not a game, this was reality.

By calling on friends I somehow managed to make a number of sales and was quite surprised to have received an award from SMI Inc., the company whose products I was "selling."

The award was a treasure chest with ten beautifully engraved quotations from Og Mandion's book *The Greatest Salesman.* On the inside cover was an inscription that read...

TO GREG WOZNICK, ONE OF THE GREATEST SALESMEN IN THE WORLD

What a preposterous statement! How very *untrue*! How very *unlike me* that inscription was. But I realized something very important. I knew that the description which was not true about me now, could become true about me... if I AFFIRMED myself to be...

ONE OF THE GREATEST SALESMAN IN THE WORLD

I purchased a small women's cosmetic mirror and glued it above the inscription. Each morning as I came into my office I lifted the lid of the treasure chest... looked into the mirror at myself... read the inscription and felt like vomiting in the chest.

The affirmation was unlike me... it was difficult to say.

No, I'm not the Worlds Greatest Salesman today... but I can tell you that with affirmations I came to enjoy selling and am proud to proclaim that "I am a *professional salesman.*" I do very little selling now... even so... I am proud to proclaim that ... "I am a professional salesman."

I continue to use affirmations on a daily basis. I affirm myself in a number of areas. Areas in which I want to continue a character strength, or to develop a deficient strength... Or perhaps I make affirmations that are just statements of a specific nature. Here are a few examples:

"I am alert, healthy, alive and sensitive."

"I have a success awareness."

"I have unlimited resources to work with."

"I think and act – and thereby succeed."

"I am great!"

"I am fantastic."

"I care about people."

"I am a loving and kind person."

"I like people... people like me."

"I am responsible."

"I enjoy life."

"I take time out to have fun."

"I take gutsy action on my goals."

"I am persuasive."

"I am enthusiastic and happy."

"I do things now."

What is there about your life that you would like to change in an easy, simple manner? What would you like to develop as a natural characteristic for you?

A healthier self-image?

An ability to handle problems?

Courage and confidence to "step out in your job or life?

An ability to meet people?

To become an accomplished speaker?

To lose weight?

To stop smoking?

To have more fun?

Or...even to be...

THE GREATEST SALESMAN IN THE WORLD?

For affirmations to be effective, we must apply certain basic principles.

1) Always use the first person singular ... "I"

2) The statement must be positive.

3) Write or state them in the present tense. ("I am." or "I do.") NOT ("I will")

4) Put them in writing.

5) Use spaced repetition... repeat... repeat... repeat and repeat... hundreds, even thousands, of times.

Spaced repetition is critical to the success of affirmations. When we consider the many hundreds of times we have heard or made a statement to ourselves that put us into a negative thought pattern, it makes sense that in order to develop a positive position about that belief, we need to give ourselves an equal, or greater number, of affirmations to off-set the negative statements.

Please be patient with yourself. Your present style of thinking may have been years in forming... expect it to take a little while to re-establish your habit of thought. It takes time for a flower to bloom; it takes time for eggs to incubate; it takes time for dust to settle... it takes time for affirmations to work.

It is important to remember that we *can* change. That we are not cast in eternal stone. We can change our habits. We can change our beliefs about ourselves. We can change our life style. We have the free moral choice to create ourselves into anything we want to be. Let's choose to be more beautiful than we are right now. Let's get to work on some of those limiting habits.

First you make your habits; then your habits make you.

WHO AM I?

I am your constant companion.

I am your greatest helper, or your heaviest burden.

I will push you onward, or drag you down to failure.

I am at your command.

Half of the tasks you do you might just as well turn over to me, and I will be able to do them quickly and correctly.

I am easily managed, you must merely be firm with me.

Show me exactly how you want something done, after a few lessons I will do it automatically.

I am the servant of all great men, and – alas – of all failures as well.

Those who are great, I have made great.

Those who are failures, I have made failures.

I am not a machine – but I work with all the precision of a machine, plus the intelligence of a man.

You may run me for profit, or run me for ruin. It makes no difference to me.

Take me. Train me. Be firm with me and I will put the world at your feet.

Be easy with me and I will destroy you.

Who am I?

I AM HABIT!

Author unknown

GET INTO THE HABIT OF LOVING YORSELF.

GET INTO THE HABIT OF BEING IN PURSUIT OF EXCELLENCE.

GET INTO THE HABIT OF DEVELOPING ALL YOUR POTENTIAL WITH POSITIVE AFFIRMATIONS.

CHAPTER 7

"If you are not getting the things out of life that you want, that you are quite capable of getting, and which you richly deserve, it may be that your goals for life are not clearly defined." Paul J. Meyer, Chairman of SMI, INC.

In the first chapter I stated that the two major obstacles to your living a fuller, richer life were:

1)   The perception you have of yourself.

2)   A lack of purpose in your life.

In the preceding chapters we have addressed the first obstacle of low perception. Let's focus our attention on the second problem, *purpose in life.*

Goal setting is absolutely essential to our growth and pursuit of excellence. Developing a healthier self-image is vital. Becoming aware of our potential for greatness is imperative.

However,   without purpose,

without goals,

without vision,

without expectations...
the development of character and potential is aimless, difficult and frustrating.

As we establish goals and purpose, life takes on a new meaning. When we set goals worthy of ourselves and worthy of our striving then growth and change take on meaning.

To simply "will" ourselves to be better brings little if any improvement. We can say...

"I want to be more loving."

"I want to be more patient."

"I want to be more successful."

"I want to be less critical."

We can make these and other desirable and sincere statements, but wanting isn't getting.

Until thought is linked to purpose – and purpose is linked to action – there is little growth or achievement. To find purpose, to establish goals and pursue them is the most zestful, motivational, life giving force available to us.

Recognize that "Want to..." statements are not affirmations. They are wishes that are allowed to drift on the ocean of life and are tossed about by every wave and ripple of circumstance. We will see that affirmations become a support system to our goals.

"Want to..." statements are at best hazy goals. Hazy goals at best give us hazy results. If you took a picture with a camera that was twenty percent out of focus, the photo finisher would probably not bother to return it to you. But if the pictures were developed, and even if the subjects were beautiful scenes or precious moments, they would be almost useless, because they would be distorted. You might even throw them away.

In the same way, our goals and dreams for life are often distorted and thrown away because they are little more than hazy "wants." They are discarded possibilities and dreams

and realities

flushed into a sea of despair, fear, doubt and worry.

I wonder how many of us have taken out "Life insurance". No, not death insurance that becomes payable to our beneficiary at the time of or death. I mean Life Insurance. Life Insurance that makes *you* the beneficiary, payable to you, now, today and tomorrow.

Have you established a "life's agenda"? Do you know what you are going to do... why you are going to do it... and how you are going to do it? Or... is each day just another day... a "wait and see" what it has in store?

We take days and weeks, and perhaps even months and years, planning and designing a blueprint for a new home. Then why do we take little, if any, time at all to develop a blueprint for our lives... the most precious, and wonderful gift we have?

The question we might ask is not... "Is there life after death"... we believe that. The question is, "Is there life after birth?" Perhaps the bedtime prayer "If I should die before I wake" should read... "If I should wake before I die."

Do you know, this moment, what are the five or ten or perhaps even twenty most important things in your life? Would you be able to recite them? Do you know them in order of priority? Do you have a plan of action for their achievement?

If so... fantastic! You can count yourself as one of the rare successful people in this nation. You are in the top three percent of achievers.

If not... that's okay... imagine how wonderful and exciting it will be to discover these life priorities. The greatest adventure you can have is to discover, or in fact to re-discover, YOU. Your greatest experience is to experience YOU. Your greatest pursuit is that of excellence.

So, if you're ready, let's start the planning for the greatest journey of your life. I guarantee that it will be the most amazing, enjoyable, challenging, exciting, and fun filled mountain climbing experience ever!

First, it is important that our *goals be written* and specific. Our mind is so marvelous that we can sort through a number of options to any question very quickly. We have had the repeated experience of sitting at a desk, or driving down the road, "thinking" or "planning". Most of the time, even after many minutes of working a problem through or mind, we fail to determine which course of action to take. We have considered several, yet without writing out the "best" option, we fail to act. And thereby we fail to achieve.

Writing crystallizes our thinking and causes us to make a positive decision... Writing is a way of giving commitment to our intention... Writing our goals in specifics keeps us on the proper course.

Writing for most of us is difficult. We procrastinate when writing almost anything, even a recipe, an address, or a letter. It may be helpful to recognize the reason for this reluctance, particularly when it involves goal setting.

Complacency

The major obstacle lies in the fact *that we may have become "satisfied"* or in a sense *"stagnant"* in our present life style. The greatest enemy of BEST is good. We may have become complacent, and may have lost our inspirational discontent with things as they are. Or, we may even feel so defeated that we may want to "give up". In either case, this is a *resistance to change.* We cling to that which is familiar even though it may not be comfortable or satisfying. We grasp for security. Mediocrity becomes our prison guard.

Monkey trappers used a very simple but ingenious method. A large but small-mouthed bottle of hard sugar cookies was put in the monkey's trail. The monkey would be overcome first by curiosity and secondly by its desire for the cookies. But after reaching in the bottle and grabbing a handful, the monkey would find that he couldn't get his hand out of the bottle. When the trapper returns, the monkey will screech and scream. It will go into a frantic hysteria, turning and twisting. But, guess what it will not do... You're right! That monkey will *not let go* of the cookie.

It would be trapped by its own desire. By refusing to release the *cookie,* it would forfeit its *freedom!*

So it is with written goals. You must be willing to let go of what you already have, and what you already are, in order to trade *good* for *best.* You cannot steal second base *and* keep your foot on first.

Procrastination

Another major impediment to our writing goals is *procrastination.* "Too busy today... tomorrow for sure..."
"Someday honey."

Fear of failure

Fear of failure causes us to resist writing goals. That's understandable. Our society has not given us permission to fail, it has only given us permission to succeed. We may have experienced ridicule, teasing, punishment for failure to meet other's expectation of ourselves. We may have been humiliated and may have even felt a sense of shame. We may have worked hard at earning the "conditional love" of parents or teachers or friends... and having failed we have known the hurt of rejection.

How sad that this "habit of thought" can trap us, even now. Throw it away... it is garbage. In every athletic contest someone loses. In every election... someone loses... Lincoln said... "My great concern is not whether you have failed, but whether you are content with your failure."

Thomas Edison had 10,000 recorded "failures" before he succeeded with the light bulb. He didn't regard them as failures... he considered them as one less possibility.

I receive many phone calls from wonderful and capable people who ask advice regarding some venture or goal they want to pursue. Usually, they have it well thought out... it looks positive... there are no "obvious" reasons for them not to pursue their vision. Yet, they hesitate and seek assurance that it is okay to do it.

It usually boils down to fear of failing. The question is not really if it is okay to have the goal – but if it is okay to fail at the goal. Certainly none of us want to fail... but I can tell you this, in any worthy venture...

YOU MUST FIRST GIVE YOURSELF
PERMISSION TO FAIL BEFORE YOU CAN
GIVE YOURSELF PERMISSION TO SUCCEED.

Low Self-Image

Another reason we hesitate to write our goals is *low self-image*. If we hold a mediocre opinion of ourselves, we set mediocre goals. Yet, we must set higher goals in order to raise our self-image. With our understanding of previous chapters, this problem should be minimal.

The last road block is that we *don't know how* to set goals. Let's eliminate that road block right now. I can do *this part* for you.

The other parts are up to you.

CHAPTER 8

As we look at the process of *goal setting,* we will want to keep in mind a few basic guidelines.

Schopenhauer said, "Man is not pushed from behind, nor pulled from in front, He is driven from within." We do not need to be "manipulated" to achieve with either the fear or incentive forms of much abused, so-called, "motivation". We are best driven from within because of who we are, and what we feel, and what we desire. Not what others may want for us – however well meaning they may be. Not what the "Jones' have or doing". The important and heartfelt issue is...

What do you want?

YOU ARE IMPORTANT. In this whole world there is not anyone as unique as you. In this whole world you are the only one you will never leave or lose... You came in alone... you will go out alone. So...

What do you want to be
> to do
>> to see
>>> to have?

What really turns you on?... What is burning inside of you? Of course, I am not talking about improper desire or selfish greed. Nor am I suggesting you set aside present "responsibilities" or the consequences of past decisions. A person came up to me after a talk on goal setting. She was excited to tell me that she was now going to get a divorce because marriage was interfering with the career that she really wanted to pursue. No, No, No, ... that would be irresponsible. Past choices and present consequences of this sort cannot be "set aside"... you still have much more latitude for achievement than you ever thought possible.

Goals must be written in a positive form. Our mind functions through mental pictures and cannot visualize a void. For example, I might say "I don't want to drive this three-year-old car anymore". Even though the goal may be worthwhile, I had said to my mind "I don't want to drive this three-year-old car anymore...I want to walk."

Or I might say, "I am going to purchase a new Cadillac this fall. It will be a two tone maroon "Seville" with the "de Elegance" interior. It will have all the extras. Stereophonic sound... automatic lights, electric seats with memory... digital control panel... and eighteen acres of hood just sweeping the way in front of me... More positive and more exciting. Don't you agree?

Driving that Cadillac sure beats walking.

You might say, "Well, that's great, but right now it is not realistic for me to drive that Seville. But I could drive a new Buick, or Oldsmobile, or Chevrolet." Fine. *Goals should be realistic, but not necessarily low.* High goals are often much easier to attain. Low goals provide a low base of motivation. High goals are more exciting, and carry greater desire and consequent action.

Critical to our success is to recognize and welcome the fact that goals *must include personality changes.* It would be unrealistic to assume that we can do better and be better by being who we are now and doing what we are doing now, in the way in which we are doing it now. This is a dog chasing its own tail... it is confusing *motion* for *progress.* Motion and progress are not the same.

Second to goal setting, personality or character change is the most imperative requirement for success. And it is the main reason for failure. If we keep on thinking the way we are thinking, and doing what we are doing, we cannot expect improvement in our life – much less climb any mountains. To continue as we like is like being a "pinwheel", it will turn only if the wind of circumstance blows against it.

As we write our goals, we will want to examine what personality traits are keeping us from our dreams. What is there in me, that is keeping me from doing what I want to do?

CHAPTER 9

Earlier, I asked, "Do you know the five, ten, twenty or more most important goals in your life?"

Would it be important to you to know them in order of priority... and to have a written plan of action that would serve as a "written guarantee" that you could have them? Of course it would. Then let's look at the procedure for developing this kind of life agenda.

Step one is fun. Take a sheet of paper and start writing.

At the top of your paper write in big letters...

'DREAM LIST"

Start writing down everything that comes to mind that you have ever wanted to have... to be... to see... to do... or to become... PLEASE don't pass judgment on your dreams... Remember... present age... present security... present conditions... present "anything" should not keep you from writing down your dreams. Most of all, *don't judge yourself.* You really have no idea how great you really are... what you are capable of doing... what you can attain... until we commit and act. PLEASE DARE TO DREAM! Don't limit yourself by past failures or present circumstance... what has happened is not as important as what we do with what has happened to us.

Don't limit yourself by what others have done or have not done.

They are not you! They have never walked in your moccasins. They don't know what makes you soar... what makes you come alive. They haven't lived your past life for you and they won't live your future for you. Don't let what others say, think, or do, cast a shadow on your personal desire for greatness. Allow no one to restrict you with his own personal limitations.

Your past negative habits of thought and conditioning should be recognized for the deceitful damaging "garbage" that they are... you may have been affirmed and conditioned by statements like...

"Save your money for a rainy day."

"Don't love too deeply you might get hurt."

"Money is the root of evil."

"Be satisfied with what you have."

or even...

"Be sure to wear clean underwear, you never know when you might have an accident, and have to go to the hospital."

Nonsense! Reaffirm yourself with positive statements, change your thinking. If you expect little you will receive little.

A daddy asked his four year old son what he wanted for Christmas... He told his son he could have *anything* he wanted.

Jimmy looked up at his father with adoring eyes and said, "Daddy, could I have that coaster wagon down at the hardware store... you know the one with the white wheels and the red box?"

His daddy smiled at him and replied, "You bet you can Jimmy, I've had a good year... it that's what you want that's what you will get."

Christmas morning Jimmy came running into the living room and looked under the tree for his "red wagon", but all he found was a "red ball".

His daddy didn't know the transmission was going to go out of his car.

The next Christmas Jimmy's daddy asked him what he wanted again. "Jimmy... this year, *for sure,* you can have anything..."

Jimmy again asked for the "red wagon".

His daddy didn't know that the washer and dryer were both going to go out.

Again, Jimmy raced into the living room on Christmas morning... looked under the tree and found... another "red ball".

And yet came a third Christmas and Daddy said, "Jimmy... I really love you, and I know I let you down... but this time you really can have anything you want."

Jimmy studied his father before replying... "Daddy do you really, really mean it this time... I can really have "anything"?

"You bet... anything" said his father.

"Gosh, in that case, daddy, can I have a "red ball"?

Sadly enough... that was the year Jimmy could have had his "red wagon". And this is the year that you can have your "RED WAGON". WRITE IT DOWN. DREAMS ARE THE CEILINGS OF REALITY... THE DREAMERS OF THE WORLD ARE THE ACHIEVERS... EVERYTHING THAT YOU SEE BEGAN AS A DREAM...

For as T. E. Lawrence so aptly puts it...

"All men dream, but not equally. They who dream by night in the dusty recesses of their mind – wake in the day to find that it is vanity;

But the dreamers of the day are dangerous men, for they act out their dreams to make it possible."

You may find that your list of dreams may fill the entire page. Or, perhaps you will have listed only a few. That is okay... Remember, these are personal. But, keep adding to your list. Your list may be as long at the end of your life as it will be now, even though you will have achieved many, many, of the dreams on your list.

Step two is to place our list in order.

By way of analogy, in our first step we have taken our camera and photographed our dreams and desires. We have placed the pictures in a box without any order.

Now we will begin to arrange our pictures into albums. We will give these albums names taken from the "wheel of life" illustration on page 35. At the top of a second page write in the following headings:

CAREER FINANCIAL SPRITUAL MENTAL
SOCIAL FAMILY PHYSICAL

Looking at our "dream list", write each dream under the appropriate column. A goal to be a better father of course would be written under family... A goal to save $1,000.00 would be written under financial... A goal to lose weight would be written under physical... and so on.

Step three is to determine the priority order for the goals listed under each heading.

Ask yourself... of all the goals I have written under (family) which goal is number one – the most important goal. On a third page with headings again listed, write the number one goal under family. Then proceed to number two... three... four, etc.

As you do this with each major area of your life, you may find it difficult – and frustrating – to sort out your priorities... stick with it. You are simply discovering that up until this point you have not really sorted out your values in the area.

Step four is to establish your overall priorities.

I asked earlier if you knew the five or ten most important things in your life, and if you knew them in order of priority. I asked if it would be important for you to know this. This step will show you how to know what is most important to you and the order of importance.

What a thrill to have this determined. What a sense of peace... of power... of purpose... you will have when you are "established"... when...

You have life insurance.

You have a Life Agenda.

You have a blueprint for life...

When you know who you are... what you stand for... where you are going... and how you are going to get there.

Step five is how are you going to get there.

On another separate sheet of paper, write the first goal you want to work on. It may not be your number one priority. This goal may be one that you feel a need to work on right now.

Write out your goal statement using keys we shared in Chapter 8.

The goal should be written and specific.

The goal should be positive.

The goal should be realistic.

Example: your goal might be to save more money. This is a *general goal...* it is a *want...* it has no deadlines. We will have no way of knowing when and if we reached this goal. You might state it like this:

"By _____ I will have increased my savings account by no less than $1,000.00."

This statement is positive, and hopefully realistic. Let's check it out. Let's examine the obstacles that stand between you and your goal.

In a separate column begin to list all the things that stand in the way of you achieving your goal. Possible obstacles might include:

- Low income.
- Present debt.
- Too much spending on non-essentials.
- Have not formed the habit of saving.
- Etc...etc...etc.

Be sure to list every obstacle that comes to mind, no matter how small or insignificant it might seem to be. There is an old proverb that says..."It is not the big things in life that give us trouble... it is the little things. You can sit on a mountain, but who wants to sit on a tack."

Next... for every obstacle, write out a solution. If we can identify the problem(s), we can identify the solution. If your obstacle is *low income* you may need to find a better paying job, or get a part time job.

If it is *present debt* you might consider consolidating your debt to reduce your monthly payment. Don't wait until you are out of debt before you start saving... start now. A part of everything you earn should be yours to keep... pay yourself first.

Too much spending on non-essentials. Change your thinking... change your personality... focus on the reason that you are saving. Is it for a new car... a vacation... security?...Does it turn you on?

Have not formed the habit of saving. Start by putting something away FIRST, even if it is ten dollars. Once you get into the HABIT of saving... it will be difficult not to save.

Notice that we have considered conditions and circumstance as well as personality traits. In every list of obstacles both will most likely appear.

Finally, for every problem and solution... write a deadline to eliminate the obstacle. This is essential. If you go through this entire process and fail to set deadlines, your entire effort will reduce itself to "wishful thinking".

You don't work on deadlines... deadlines work on you. We somehow get the energy and the time... when deadlines are approaching... If you think otherwise, consider the income tax deadline... or the time in school when you were given three weeks to write a term paper. When did you do it? Right, the last few days, or the last night... you may have been writing even as the teacher came down the row to pick up your paper. Deadlines work on you!

By this time you may be saying... "This is too involved." "This is too much like work." "I'm really too busy." "I am sure it can work for others, but I don't think it will work for me." "Someday" I am going to take the time to really do this...

"Someday"
"Someday"
"Someday"

WHY NOT THIS DAY!

You will be amazed to find that goals you wrote for completion a year from now, you will accomplish in six or seven months... Dreams that you thought were "Red Wagons", and were reserved for the "few who made it", will be yours. You will travel where you never thought possible.

"You will see things you never thought you would see."

"You will have things you never thought you would have."

"You will become the kind of person you always wanted to be."

Wouldn't you agree that it would be worth... just a few minutes a day... a few minutes per week to:

"GET THE THINGS OUT OF LIFE THAT YOU WANT, THAT YOU ARE QUITE CAPABLE OF GETTING, AND WHICH YOU RICHLY DESERVE."

CHAPTER 10

The universe is still in a creation process. All things are in the process of change...

> Mountains are wearing down
> Oceans are filling up
> Sand is shifting
> Volcanoes are erupting
> The earth is "quaking"
> Man is taller

And *you* are not the same today as you were yesterday.

> Your thoughts
> Your food
> Your actions
> Your feelings

Your experiences have made you different.

You are still being created! And, you will not be the same tomorrow as you are today. Creative change is in constant motion like the waves against a sea shore. But, what is to be created, unlike the waves washing against the sea shore, is within your power to control and direct.

While the creative process continues in motion,
The principles that Govern

Regulate

Direct

Control

The process are   Fixed

Firm

Dependable

Constant

Workable

Available

As you understand and apply this principle of belief to your self-image, and to your goals, you will find it to be the magnifier and accelerator to your dreams.

You can change...

Anxiety to peach
Worry to security
Poverty to wealth
Debt to financial freedom
Broken relationships to happy ones
Failure to success
Confusion to purpose

DREAMS TO REALITY

Let's examine the meaning of the two words POWER AND BELIEF.

Words are alive and active.
Words have creative power.
Words are the tools of imagination
Words are the bricks of construction.

The work POWER comes from the Greek word *dynamous,* the root word for *'dynamite'.* It is a dynamite word. It is a powerful, explosive action.

Webster defines POWER as "a force or energy used to do work...

a physical might...

a mental or moral vigor

a spiritual vigor."

The word BELIEF is the mental act, condition, or habit of placing trust or confidence in a person or thing; we also call it FAITH.

Belief is a strong conviction. Belief is faith that goes beyond fact, it is futuristic.

"if thou canst believe, all things are possible to him who believes." *Mark* 9:23

"As thou hast believed, so be it done unto you."
Matthew 8:13

The word belief as we view it here is different than the world's belief which says "Seeing is believing." The belief we are speaking of says *"Believing is seeing."*

Believing is a vision...

a dream...

a fantasy...

held out in belief's positive expectancy until it is accomplished. That is motivation.

So the "power of belief" that we want to apply to our dreams, our goals, our life is not based upon fact. We accept as fact that when we mail a letter it will arrive in a certain number of days. We accept as fact that if we travel one-hundred miles at fifty miles per hour we will arrive in two hours... this is not belief as we want to understand it.

The belief we are "taking hold of" requires no...

Proof

Prior facts

Logic

Past experience.

We are speaking of the belief in the moon flight. We are speaking of the belief of the Wright brothers at Kitty Hawk. Imagine their belief in a machine that was heavier than air — yet a machine that could fly. It had never been done before... no previous experience... no previous proof... and quite 'illogical'.

I think of Samuel Morris, whose friends appeared in congress to request a $30,000.00 appropriation to stretch a wire so that Morris could send *messages by wire*. Congress scoffed and said, "Why not build a railroad from here to the moon instead."

I think of Marconi whose "friends" tried to commit him to an insane asylum because of his *belief* in the possibility of sending a *wireless message*.

I share this to encourage you to *believe* in the reality of your dreams... regardless how seemingly "impossible" they may seem. Whether or not you have ever "done this before". No matter what other people may say... or think... or do.

William James said, "The one thing that will guarantee the successful outcome of even the most doubtful undertaking, is belief in the beginning that you can do it."

Belief is the driver that joins faith with action to get what you richly deserve from life. Successful people have great belief that appears as a "calm assurance" to the viewer.

Belief is a...
Fixed...
Firm...
Dependable...
Constant...
Workable...
Available...
Principle that is ready to work for you.

I cannot fly... no matter how fast or hard I flap my arms... or how high I jump..., or how fast I run... or how high a building I choose from which to jump.

If I want to fly... I must understand and *apply certain principles*. I must apply the principles of lift, or aerodynamics. I understand the law of gravity... I accept the fact that a falling body will drop at the rate of 16 feet per second squared until it reaches maximum velocity. It works this way even if you don't believe it. It is a fixed law of nature.

When we apply the principles of aerodynamics and are able to overcome the law of gravity and fly... the laws that govern flight do not neutralize or nullify the laws that govern gravity... it simply allows us to "rise above" it. If you don't believe it... step out of a plane at 30,000 feet altitude and you will quickly notice that the law of gravity is back in control.

The power of belief is like the principle of aerodynamics. It helps you to rise above the obstacles that would pull you down, and would keep you where you are. It gives you the wings of an eagle. You can soar above the mundane, above the muddles, above the problems and the negative thinking with its negative belief and its negative results.

In the next chapter we will examine the principles and the laws that operate continually in the *power of belief.*

CHAPTER 11

The laws that govern the power of belief are as real as the laws of physics. But, unlike the laws of physics, we cannot observe them in a controlled laboratory setting, and we are seldom keeping them in constant positive usage. So the results are not obviously absolute or conclusive.

Even so, they can be observed in the reality of life's laboratory. And the degree of their success will be in direct proportion to the accuracy of their application.

THE LAW OF ATTRACTION

Your mental attitude regulates the law of attraction. You cannot draw to yourself more than you are – more than the thoughts you think... the habits you have formed, and the possibilities you imagine.

We are the product of the dominating thoughts that occupy our minds. The reality of who you are today had its roots in the thought regulated actions of yesterday. You are constantly becoming what you think.

> When you change what you think...
> you change who you are.
> When you change who you are...
> you change what you think.

We must accept responsibility for our thinking. We cannot pass the consequences of our thinking off on others. And yet, whose thoughts *are* controlling and forming *your* tomorrows...your thoughts, or those of other people?

Why not choose to build your life on your own original thought... your own dreams... your own desires? Why accept someone else's thinking for your life. To accept anyone else's life pattern or goals is to accept "second hand junk" – when you have the limitless options of your own unique "originals"!

Get in control. Decide who you are, and decide what you want to be. The law of attraction is limited by our own self-image. You cannot change what is happening "out there" until you change what is happening *"in here"*. As you believe, let it be done unto you. You are great... believe it.

> You have great potential... believe it.
> You are unique in all this world... believe it.
> You have unlimited ability... believe it.
> You are capable of living a life of
> Joy and abundance... BELIEVE IT.

SUCCESS IS WHAT WE ARE FROM THE INSIDE TO
THE OUTSIDE.

When you change the inside, you *do* change the
outside. Your mental attitude will attract to itself the
conditions and circumstances that correspond to its present
state of mind.

Remember, you cannot magnetize to yourself more
than you are. A weak self-image is like a weak radio
sending signals to your "ship". The "ship" that is out there
somewhere "waiting to come in". The ship is there, and it
does want to come in. But, by the nature of your self-image,
and lack of belief, the signal isn't clear enough to respond.
It is just "wishful thinking".

There is a graveyard of ships that "never came in".
They were left to drift on a sea of negative self-images and
attitudes. You cannot bring to yourself anything that your
mind does not believe is possible for you. People who
believe otherwise buy lottery tickets and chances on prizes,
a substitute for belief. It is called "dumb luck". DON'T
COUNT ON IT.

You don't get what you want... you get what you
believe is possible for you. Perhaps your past experience is
one of losing... or failure. This past experience has given
you doubt and un-belief in yourself. You may be drawing
to yourself the exact conditions that correspond to this
unwanted nature. Unwanted nature... unwanted
conditions...

For example:

You say to yourself, "I want to earn $50,000 a year" or... "I want to lose weight."

"I want to own my own business."

"I want to win the gold medal."

You have said this to yourself time and time again... and now you are determined to do it.

Even as you make this very positive statement, a little voice called the subconscious says, "Oh yea? I've heard that before. Here we go again. We'll never make it."

That is an expression of a losing self-image, and negative thinking. It is also *reality*. But it is only *reality of the past*. With the tools and the procedures you are receiving you can change that reality of the past. You may find it easier to start with smaller goals – smaller victories – getting the positive you into the habit or winning.

YOU ARE A WINNER... THE FACTS DON'T COUNT.

Remember that present facts don't count – not in BELIEF.

If you dream

    and decide

    and commit

    and put this force behind it

YOU CAN DO IT.

GO FOR IT.

Facts didn't count for Edison when he had 10,000 failures. Facts didn't count for the Wright Brothers. Or Morris. Or Marconi. And they don't need to count for you. If you were playing basketball and were fifty points behind at half time... but knew you were going to win... THE FACTS WOULD NOT COUNT!

Blow the soot out of your sub-conscious... If your dream machine is broken, get it RE-CONDITIONED. When you tell your sub-conscious that you are going to do it with a belief attitude it will say, "YIPPEE... LET'S GO DO IT!" It will be jumping with joy to be on the right track. It really will!

Feel great about your new abundance... You will be creating new, wonderful, and original things. And the more you have – the more you have to give. No one will have less because you have more! Other people will have more *because* you have more. How many people do you support when you are able to buy a new car? A new home? A new suit?

What blessings do you receive when you give? You will be unable to give your abundance away... it returns to you full measure, pressed down, and running over. Go ahead, try it... start now.

IMAGINATION

Imagination is a delivery system that helps you visualize *your kind* of world into existence.

Imagination is a supply bridge over which arrive the best things of life. It is a ladder to the stars. A telescope of your future. It is a preview of coming events. Your coming events.

Without this prerequisite to growth we repeat our life's condition with modest and insignificant change. We may find ourselves working simply to avoid pain, or perhaps to gain a moment of pleasure.

Without imagination we become myopic, looking at life though blurred and narrow vision. We become mummified – musty. We walk with our eyes to the ground

> backs bent
> shoulders stooped
> legs weary
> spirits troubled

sliding our tired feet over pieces of fragmented and trampled dreams.

We rationalize our life away with excuses, or even with blaming. We dull our emotions... kill our desires. We stop listening to the voice of heart urging us on to greatness.

We dare not dream the impossible dream. We dare not march to the beat of our own stirring drum. We may even become like a robot wound up each morning, only to be unwound again by night time.

THIS IS NOT WHAT YOU WERE BORN FOR. What will you say to the Master when He asks you for an accounting of the five, or two, or even one thousand talents He gave you? Will you say, "Here Master, I have doubled it."?

Will He say, "Good and faithful servant, because you have been faithful in little things I shall give you even more."?

Or, will you say this? "Here Master... I knew you would be demanding of what you gave me, so I hid my talents under a rock... I didn't use them... here they are no more, but no less, than what you gave me."

What will He say? You know very well what he will say.

"Do you mean that you did nothing with the talent I gave you?—You allowed it just to gather dust? – You didn't bother to even gain interest on it?"

Isn't it amazing that he took the one-thousand and gave it to the one who had five? And then He said, "For he who has much, even more shall be given to him. And he who has little, even that shall be taken away from him."

Use your imagination, put it to work for you. Imagination is not reserved for a few people. It is not limited to the artist, the architect, the writer, the musician. It is available to all. And it stands ready for use by whoever wants to exercise it. We were born with a vivid imagination. Remember when you played:

Cowboys
Cops and robbers
House
Doctor
Nurse
Teacher
Preacher
Astronaut
President
Hero

Remember when you...

Won the Miss America Beauty Contest
Flew the swiftest plane
Sang with your favorite group
Starred in a famous movie
Rode the meanest horse
Sank the winning basket
Climbed the *highest mountain?*

Remember when...

The Universe was your playground.
Eternity was your clock... and
Imagination was your best friend.
What happened to this best friend? Was this childhood
friend discarded like:

a broken wagon
a busted doll
a punctured ball

Was it all empty? Was it shouting down a rain barrel... only
to hear a brief echo return and then disappear? Forever?

Are dreams wasted on childhood? Did we spend
our time in worthless... wasted... non-redeemable energy?
Or, were they, in fact, exercises?
Exercises in POSSIBILITIES
POTENTIALS
DREAMS
REALITY?
Did that imagination have significance?
Did it have meaning – value – substance—purpose?

Did being "undisciplined" make it useless and undesirable?

What happened to this *substance of life?* Where did it go?

It was conditioned out of us. We were told not to dream. Not to have such a "wild imagination". We were told to be realistic... We were told that we were sevens – or eights – or ones.

Recapture this joy of your youth. Revitalize this essential of imagination and creativity. Remember that we are not speaking of the drifting form of imagination called day dreaming. We are speaking of positive and directed imagination that requires mental labor – that requires discipline. Let it create, and stimulate, and draw to you all that you want to be... to have... to see... to do... to become.

> "When I examine myself, and my methods of thought, I come to the conclusion that the gift of fantasy has meant more to me than my talent for absorbing positive knowledge."
>
> Albert Einstein

VISUALIZATION

"Whatever you vividly imagine, ardently desire and enthusiastically act upon, must inevitably come to pass." Paul J. Meyer

When you have determined your dream, and have built your image to attract the dream, and then have imagined your possibilities – your next step is to "picturize" the dream.

That trip to Hawaii

That new boat
That new job
That new look.

Picture and visualize it happening. Picture yourself at that next convention... the banquet room is packed full. Background music is playing "Dream the Impossible Dream." The music has been softened, and the President steps to the podium at the head table. He is smiling because he knows that the suspense is building as the audience awaits his announcement of the top award of the year... the President's Trophy.

He pauses at the microphone, then looks slowly, quietly around the room. You are hoping he will glance at you and in his eyes you might see a signal that the winner is – you.

The President doesn't look at you... your heart sinks. But your heart keeps pounding out the drum beat of expectation. Finally...

"I am delighted to announce the award of the President's Trophy to someone who has shown high purpose and great integrity. A person who has achieved and attained new records, and whom I have come to respect and admire. Ladies and gentlemen, it pleases me to award this trophy to... **Your name.** He has awarded the President's Trophy to you! The crowd sits quietly for a moment... You sit shocked, absorbing the moment. Then the audience rises to its feet to applaud. To applaud *you* – for who you are – and for what you have achieved...

That is *visualization.*

PICTURE YOURSELF... as you want to be
AFFIRM YOURSELF... as you want to become.

Visualization is the process of making mental pictures of material things... experiences... feeling that thrill of its achievement. It is experiencing part of the event before it happens... it is an appetizer...

It is more than that. Visualization begins to bring things to us... Yes, it begins to bring the things *we want* to us. It is not so much that we always "pursue" our goals; it is that our goals began to pursue us.

Goals must be pictured mentally before they can be accomplished materially. It is a cause and effect principle. If there is no demand... if there is no "specific request", there is no purpose in providing the supply.

LOOK AT YOUR GOAL:

> PICTURE IT
> FEEL IT
> EXPERIENCE IT
> RECEIVE IT

GO AHEAD – CLIMB THE
HIGHEST MOUNTAIN!

SUPPLEMENT

A

Message

Of

Love

PREFACE

In 1985 while in prayer, Mereece was inspired to write this message to be given to each of our sixteen grandchildren on their sixteenth birthday.

It was filed away and forgotten until 1996.

Mereece had a carotid artery by-pass to the brain in 1995 and lost much of her speaking ability. This letter has special meaning because this is the message she would have given to each of her grandchildren in a personal heart-to-heart talk

Never stop improving your knowledge and deepening your perception so that you can always recognize what is best.

This will help you become pure and blameless, and prepare you for the Day of Christ, when you will reach the perfect goodness which Jesus Christ produces in us for the glory and praise of God.

– Philippians 1:9-11

...And besides, it is a much better way to live life. Keep your mind on good and excellence.

Look towards what is right.
Whenever you have a choice, choose rightness.
Never taking the easy way unless it is the right way.

In fact, when in doubt as to what is right to do ... look to the hardest thing to do ... you'll usually find it there.

It will increase your self-evaluation ... your worth in your own eyes. Then, as you look back, the memories you live with ... always ... will be better than ashes, less painful, more pleasing and uplifting.

Don't try to evade life's problems. You might as well learn to deal with them in a noble way for they will always be cropping up all life long.

Whenever you have a choice, choose rightness ... the consequences are easier to bear.

Learn to turn and look life's problems straight in the eye ... don't turn your back and run or you'll be pursued by them all your life.

The tiger problems in your life will always be stalking you. You feel it in the darkness at your back. Turn and face it down ... challenge it, defeat it, run it off.

It really is a paper tiger, a pussy cat, that only grows strong in your fear. Otherwise dishonesty and denial will be your companions ... existing in your running ... your escape trappings always ready to deceive ... excuse ... justify ... and accuse others.

Always be honest with yourself. You are your most faithful friend. You will <u>never</u> leave you in this life and the next. So be faithful and honest and kind to yourself. God entrusted you to you to create something noble and worthy.

Don't play games with yourself that will deceive you. Have courage with yourself. Don't desert or ignore your best friend ... You. Be tough if you have to be with yourself, but be truthful. You deserve truth. Look always for <u>truth</u> that your character can use as a basis for building the life's principles that you set for yourself. Make a list of life principles that you will live by ... that you will <u>fight</u> to live by ... that you will stand on ... resisting all that would try to rob you and bring you down to their troubled, tangled mind set.

If you decide the standards you will live by ... people will not be able to confuse you. You'll have more mental and emotional energy left to be able to get on with life. As scripture says: You'll be able to get on with more mature food instead of continually needing to eat pabulum.

It will give you a sense of direction. When all around you may be stumbling and bewildered and tossed this way and that. When all around you are depending on others:

> *to make sense of things for them*
> *to give existence meaning*
> *to feel worthy*
> *to give them activity captivating enough to*
> *   provide a false life to hide in*
> *to provide excuses for them.*

Instead lean on your <u>own understanding</u>. Think clearly, freed from chemical dependencies that cloud the mind... free from sin that entraps and distorts how we view life, truly alive and alert and <u>free</u> to make clear decisions.

Seek your own way with...

> *Your Heavenly Father caring and providing*
> *Jesus, your savior and teacher*
> *The Holy Spirit as your <u>trusted</u> companion.*

You are always on life's threshold but most especially now. God gave you freedom of choice. Don't enslave yourself again. Inform yourself... exercise your choice... choose well... choose the best... choose excellence. Excellence should not be measured in material things but always measured in who you are inside.

When you prepare something... what you put in to it and the care with which you prepared it determines the outcome. The same is true of most everything but most especially your character.

You are old enough now to begin to choose with some wisdom what goes into your character. Some of the things you will choose... is to rebuild areas that you see got off to a wrong start... never give up the struggle for excellence and, believe me, it can be a wrestling match.

*<u>Never</u> giving up... pursuing excellence... is in itself,
Character building.*

Good character is like a muscle. It must be exercised so it will grow stronger. Each of us has good character muscle that leads to excellence and poor character muscle that leads to poverty. It is surprising how little it takes before you began to feel drawn one way or the other. We must <u>keep</u> in <u>good</u> so we can give ourselves a good fighting chance.

Be kind to your dear, sweet mind, remembering what you put into it will be with you for a life time. If not on a conscious level but always influencing your every day.

When self pity or depression sneak up on you and climb up on your back for a free joy ride, turn around and bite them... scare them off. Have nothing to do with them. Tell them to get out of your mind... then go do something <u>right</u>, <u>good</u> or <u>beautiful</u>, and <u>treat yourself</u> kindly.

Guilt has its place so we can recognize sin and ask forgiveness... then say to guilt, "Thank you very much. You've been a great help. I'm taking care of things the best I can... so please, back off and leave the rest to My Heavenly Father and me." Guilt can be a friend to your dear, sweet mind but it is not to move in and take over. It is only to be used to your advantage. It is only a tool for correction, not a life's companion. Use it for the purpose it is intended (for recognition and adjustment) not for paddle board.

Value yourself and <u>love</u> yourself as your Heavenly Father does... truly appreciate His creation in you and pat yourself on the back for all the good decisions and actions of your life. Be <u>honest</u> with yourself. Take credit for all the good you've placed in your life.

Some unhappiness is natural... happiness is different than joy. Happiness is an effect from without... dependent on events from without one's self. Joy is from within and is not dependent on life's circumstances but an internal self worth. Jesus gives us joy... an eternal sense of well being.

Sadness has its place but must never master us. Grief has its time but must know when its time is up and <u>must</u> be made to give way to a more life giving mind set.

Don't be afraid of loneliness. It will pass in and out of your life continually. Understand it... learn to handle it.

> *Remember to be kind to your dear, sweet mind.*
> *It is your companion for all eternity.*
> *In this life you are responsible for it.*
> *Fill it with truth and excellence.*
> *After death it will be brought to perfection by*
>   *Our Heavenly Father.*

Change what you can in life to conform with your standard. Pray for what you cannot... do not accept it... but tolerate it only out of necessity... never grow comfortable with it but do come to peace.

Bless you all your life. Live in the richness of the Spirit, in Christ Jesus. Go for it. Bless God for the life He's given you.

Your grandmother,

Mereece Woznick

54197176R00069

Made in the USA
Lexington, KY
05 August 2016